# FRANK MILLER ★ DAVE GIBBONS

# GIVE ME
# LIBERTY ™

DARK · HORSE · COMICS ®

**The authors gratefully acknowledge Robin Smith for coloring the illustrations.**

Mike Richardson • publisher
Neil Hankerson • executive vice president
David Scroggy • vice president of publishing
Lou Bank • vice president of sales & marketing
Andy Karabatsos • vice president of finance
Mark Anderson • general counsel
Diana Schutz • editor in chief
Randy Stradley • creative director
Cindy Marks • director of production & design
Mark Cox • art director
Chris Creviston • director of accounting
Michael Martens • marketing director
Tod Borleske • sales and licensing director
Mark Ellington • director of operations
Dale LaFountain • director of m.i.s.

Published by Dark Horse Comics
10956 SE Main Street
Milwaukie, OR 97222

Second trade paperback edition: December 1994
ISBN: 1-56971-067-8

First hardcover limited edition: January 1995
ISBN: 1-56971-045-7

2 4 6 8 10 9 7 5 3 1
Printed in Canada

# I KNOW NOT WHAT COURSE OTHERS MAY TAKE BUT - AS FOR ME - GIVE ME LIBERTY OR GIVE ME DEATH

## PATRICK HENRY (1775)

# 1: HOMES & GARDENS

KREK

BASTARD--

YEAR LATER, THAT WAS THE YEAR MY *FATHER* DIED.

YEAR THE *PRESIDENT* WAS ELECTED.

FOR THE *FIRST* TIME.

HHNGG

DAD DIED IN A *PROTEST* AGAINST THE *GREEN*.

DAD SAID THE GREEN'S A *PRISON* FOR PEOPLE WHO HAVEN'T DONE ANYTHING *WRONG*.

CABRINI GREEN

LOWER INCOME HOUSING FACILITY

CHICAGO, ILLINOIS

THEY CALL IT *SOCIAL WELFARE* BUT DAD CALLS IT A *PRISON*.

JOHN WASHINGTON
1955
1996

IT'S GOT *BARBED WIRE* LIKE A PRISON. AND THEY *SHOOT* YOU IF YOU TRY TO GET *OUT*.

NOBODY EVER GETS OUT. NOT EVEN WHEN THEY'RE DEAD.

DAD NEVER GOT OUT OF THE GREEN.

2000

HELL YES

2001

I CAN'T SLEEP.

IT'S NOT THE NOISE. THERE ISN'T MUCH NOISE TONIGHT.

AIR'S BETTER TONIGHT. NOT MUCH COUGHING.

DICKENS, BUT HE ALWAYS COUGHS.

WHUP WHUP

WHUP

WHUP

WHUP

WHUP

WHUP

WHUP

DICKENS, AND THE GROWNUPS.
THE GROWNUPS ALWAYS COUGH.

THERE'S NO **STREETS** IN THE GREEN.

NO **CARS** SO NO **STREETS**.

JUST SIDEWALKS AND SIDEWALKS AND THE **TUBE** IF YOU'RE TOO **OLD** TO **WALK** OR IF YOU'RE **CRAZY** ENOUGH TO TAKE THE **TUBE**.

SHIT

GOD LOVES

GOD LOVES

ON MY WAY TO **SCHOOL** AND **THUNDERBALLS** SEES ME **ALONE**.

DRESSED LIKE A **BOY** LIKE ALWAYS.

CRAZY TO DRESS LIKE A GIRL.

GOD LOVES

DRESS LIKE A **BOY** BUT I GUESS IT DOESN'T FOOL **THUNDERBALLS**.

GIVE ME ANY **SHIT** I FUCKING **KILL** YOU.

I DON'T GIVE HIM ANY SHIT.

THUNDERBALLS TAKES ME TO THE GYMNASIUM AND ON THE WAY I ALMOST THROW UP.

TAKES ME RIGHT PAST THE *ICE MAN*. RIGHT PAST HIM AND I SWEAR THE ICE MAN LOOKS RIGHT AT ME FOR A SECOND.

THE *POPE* PULLS MY *PANTS* DOWN AND STARTS YELLING AT THUNDERBALLS.

SHOULD'VE FUCKING *KNOWN* YOU'D FUCK ME *UP* TEE-BALLS YOU FUCKING *IDIOT* --

NFF

--BUT YOU *DIDN'T* FUCKING FUCK ME UP-- *NO* MOTHERFUCKER FUCKS THE FUCKING *POPE* UP--

CHINKK

*LOOKED* BUTCH, MAN-- SHE *LOOKED* LIKE A *BOY*, MAN --

YOU STILL *HERE* ?

NEVER SAW THUNDERBALLS AGAIN AFTER THAT.

REXALL?

CAN'T WATCH TV FOR **TEN MINUTES** WITHOUT SEEING THAT **COMMERCIAL**. ALWAYS REMINDS ME HOW MOM **HATES** IT...

CAN'T YOU **FEEL** IT?

THERE'S A NEW **SPIRIT** SWEEPING THROUGH AMERICA...A NEW **HOPE**...

...AND NEW **OPPOR-TUNITIES** -- FOR **EVERY** AMERICAN

WANT A **GOOD** JOB? **FREE** COLLEGE EDUCATION?

ADVENTURE IN EXOTIC LANDS?

AND PLENTY OF EXCITEMENT RIGHT HERE AT HOME?

JOIN THE TEAM. JOIN PAX, THE PEACE FORCE--FOR AMERICA--AND FOR YOU.

YOU'LL NEVER NEED ANOTHER JOB.

...HATES THE PEACE FORCE BECAUSE MY BROTHER KEN SIGNED UP WITH THEM AND NEVER CAME HOME. MIGHT BE DEAD.

P·A·X

DAMN...

LEAST HE GOT OUT...

...THAT'S WHAT'S SO WEIRD ABOUT DONALD. HOW HE GOT IN.

HE VOLUNTEERED.

DONALD'S REAL NICE. HE'S A TEACHER FROM OUTSIDE AND HE SHOWS ME HOW TO USE THE COMPUTERS BETTER.

NOBODY FORCED HIM INTO THE GREEN. HE VOLUNTEERED. HE DOESN'T ACT CRAZY, BUT HE VOLUNTEERED.

OH, THIS--ON MY WAY OUT LAST NIGHT AND ONE OF THE GUARDS AT THE GATE HITS ME UP FOR MONEY.

I TOLD HIM WHERE TO GO, AND, WELL...DON'T WORRY. I REPORTED HIM.

YOU OUGHT TO GET OUT OF THE GREEN, DONALD. YOU CAN SO YOU OUGHT TO.

AND WHERE WOULD THAT LEAVE MY FAVORITE STUDENT?

HE BRINGS SANDWICHES FROM OUTSIDE.

THEY TASTE GREAT.

# 2008

WHEN IT *SLEETS* THE *METAL* ON THE *ROOF* SOUNDS LIKE ABOUT A *MILLION* STEEL DRUMS AND GIVES EVERYBODY A *HEADACHE*.

THEN IT *MELTS*.

WITH THE *HELICOPTERS* ALWAYS AROUND, THEY'RE NOT WORRIED ABOUT THE *ROOF* SO NOBODY'S FIXED THE *SEAMS* SINCE BEFORE I WAS *BORN*.

JUST TRY STAYING DRY ON THE SIDEWALKS.

OR ANYWHERE ELSE.

NONE OF THE ROOFS ARE ANY GOOD ANYWHERE.

NONE OF THEM.

DONALD

NEVER KNEW DONALD HAD A SWITCHBLADE.

NFF

DONALD

HNH ?

THNKK

HGGN

SKRNCHH

KLIK
KIK
KLIK

KIK
KIK

HNFF

KIK
KIK KLIK
KIK

HREGG

... NOT RIGHT *AWAY*--

EGGS

STRAIGHT UP EGGS

GOD *DAMN* IT-- HOLD HER *STILL* FOR CHRIST'S SAKE--

--AND BY THE TIME I *CAN* TALK AND I *CAN* STOP MY LEGS AND ARMS FROM TWITCHING AND I *CAN*-- I *CAN* STOP IT--

--ALL BY *MYSELF*--

--BY THE TIME I'M *ALL RIGHT*--

--BY THEN I HEAR THEM *TALKING* ABOUT TAKING ME *AWAY*--

--AWAY-- TO A *STATE FACILITY*

--OUT OF THE GREEN--

--*OUT OF THE GREEN* --IT BREAKS MOM'S *HEART* TO SEE ME ACTING LIKE I'M *STUPID* AND *CRAZY* -- BUT THERE'S NO WAY TO *TELL* HER--

--NO WAY TO *TELL* HER--

--NO WAY TO *TELL* HER--

--NO WAY--

--WAY TO --

--WWYYTT...

WAY *OUT* OF THE *GREEN*

WHATEVER THEY FEED ME, I'LL GET

OUT

I'LL GET OUT

# 2009

LEMMEE-- LEMMEE--

--HK--

LEMMEE--

STATE CORRECTIONAL FACILITY THE CRIMINALLY INSANE

MAN OUT THERE'S *CRAZY*

WANTS TO GET BACK *IN*

BACK UNDER *WATER*

NO *AIR* HERE JUST *WATER* BUT YOU CAN

CAN BREATHE IT ANYWAY

MOSTLY SIT BY MYSELF AND IGNORE THE CURRENTS

# MEATRACK

JANUARY 2009 • $12.95

**GIRLS OF THE PEACE FORCE**

WHAT WE'RE FIGHTING FOR

THE MAN WHO WOULD BE *Elvis* EXCLUSIVE INTERVIEW

PEPPER REXALL'S WAR ON PORN

**STEAMY SOFTWARE**
THIS YEAR'S HOTTEST PROGRAMS

JESUS CHRIST--

--MEKKELSON I'LL HAVE YOUR ASS FOR THIS...

GOD DAMN IT

SHE CAN HEAR ME THINK

THEY'RE MEAN

BUT THE MEANEST

PRETTY

IS WHEN THEY THROW ME OUT

## SDI Disaster

It was aimed at Libya — but the laser cannon struck the oil-rich desert of Saudi Arabia. In the greatest environmental disaster of the century, the desert is ablaze. The sky is black over the Middle East — and our closest ally may now be America's deadliest enemy. **International: Page 34**

*Ally turned enemy: King Xassad*

## Are The Good Times Over?

*A skyrocketing deficit and plummeting stock market raise new doubts about Rexonomics*

The Wall Street panic continues. Experts talk of a collapse of the world economy — and blame the economic policies of a presidency already plagued by growing civil unrest and condemnation by the United Nations. Is Rexall's reign finished? How bad will it get? Will we recover? **National Affairs: Page 18**

## Death Clouds

The flames are a quarter mile high, a blazing field the size of Connecticut. But environmentalists warn that the real danger lies in the jet black smoke — predicting death in the many thousands worldwide as massive lethal clouds circle the earth. **Environment: Page 53**

*This smoke will bring death to thousands, experts say*

## Apache Warlord

*On the Warpath*

Two years ago his people suffered from unspeakable poverty and an 89% alcoholism rate. The youthful, charismatic Chief Redfeather has galvanised Apache cultural pride. But can he fulfill his promise to make the Apache Nation economically self-sufficient? **Nation: Page 20**

*Left behind: America's mentally ill*

## Out in the Cold

Economic belt tightening is roughest on those who can't vote — an estimated 200,000 patients have been kicked out of U.S. mental institutions following recent budget cuts. How will they survive? THISWEEK looks at the most pathetic victims of hard times. **Lifestyle: Page 87**

### National Affairs
Nightmare on Wall Street 18
Chief Redfeather 20
Riots rock the housing
  projects 21
Is PAX constitutional?
  The debate drags on 22
Will Rexall resign? 24
New look for the
  Ku Klux Klan 29
Planned communities and
  civil rights 33

### International
SDI disaster
  How did it happen 34
  Saudis vow revenge 34
  World leaders condemn
  U.S. 36
Central America
  Children at War 37
  Ambush in Managua 37
No hope for summit? 41
Australia's Aborigine
  revolt 42
Vatican sex scandal 44

### Environment
Darkness at noon
  How long will it last? 49
  Death clouds 53
Our vanishing rain forests 55
Tattered ozone layer 56
Life in the Antarctic
  Desert 56
New virus update 57

### Litigation
Shleck loses again 58
The fight for porn
  software 62
Arizona vs. Texas
  no end in sight 64

### Science
Space cannons too big to
  work? 70
China's new initiative 72
Radioactive farming 73
Computer telepathy 74
Zero gravity surgery 76

### Lifestyle
**Family:** Polygamy is back 78
**Television:** The new sex
  explosion 81
**Fashion:** The PAX look 83
**Sex:** Impotence rate soars 85
**Survival:** Our abandoned
  mentally ill 87

### Departments
Periscope 5
My Turn 11
The Mail 13
Perspectives 17
Newsmakers 89
Transition 90
Buzz Chernencko 92

Cover:*Illustration by Ron Cull — THISWEEK*

PFFT

GOGGGGHHKK

SETTLE DOWN... IT'S JUST A TRANQUILIZER...

SON OF A BITCH...

THE WHITE SUITS...

OH CHRIST

YAAAAA

--SON OF A BITCH--

WHAT...?

OH, NO.OH JESUS...

--THE WHITE SUITS --THEY ACT LIKE THEY'LL HELP YOU --

--BUT THEY JUST KILL--

--THEY JUST KILL

BITCH I'LL KILL YOU--

BITCH-- ALMOST TORE MY BALLS OFF --KILL YOU--

CHRIST DON'T LET HER --NFF

NO YOU BASTARDS --FUCKING MURDERERS --

WHAT'S...?

WHFFN

HHNFF?

YOU'LL GET YOUR SHOT, YOU CRAZY BITCH--

SKREKK

--COME AND GET--

--GGLAAGGHH

INSIDE THE *SUIT*--THERE'S A *MAN*--

INSIDE-- THERE'S A *FACE*--

HHNGAAAHH

HK--

HK--

HK--

HK--

HK--

CREDIT CARDS-- A *BANK* CARD-- THE KIND YOU USE IN THOSE *MACHINES* ON THE *STREET*--

--THOSE *COMPUTERS* ON THE *STREET* THAT *ANYBODY* CAN GET INTO --IF THEY'VE GOT A *CARD*--

YOUR BALANCE:

$32.56

TAK TAK

TAK TAK TAK

YOUR BALANCE:

$32,560.00

KCHAK

KCHAK

KCHAK

DECEMBER 27, 2009

$8.95

# ERA

## MAN OF THE YEAR

**Howard Johnson Nissen**
**President of the United States**

# How

## History's Unlikeliest President Saves the Soul of America

May 5, 2009: A Saudi Arabian firebomb reduces the White House to a blazing shell, incapacitating President Rexall and incinerating Vice President Cargo, Attorney General Sphincter, and every member of the scandal-plagued Rexall Cabinet. Every member but one.

Acting Secretary of Agriculture Howard Johnson Nissen, home in bed with a hundred and two degree fever, rose from his bed and reached for the ringing telephone — and found himself holding the highest office in the land.

A liberal democrat only momentarily boosted into the Cabinet position by the death two weeks earlier of Secretary Placebo, Nissen had fully expected the call would end his career. It was no secret that Rexall was displeased with his militant environmentalism.

While Rexall languished in a coma from which he has yet to recover, the first new chief executive in thirteen years wasted no time in reviving America's

## SWORDS INTO PLOWSHARES

Nissen ends months of terror at home and abroad, making peace with the Apache Nation [right], negotiating the Swords into Plowshares Disarmament Treaty with Soviet Premier Jackoff [above], and commits America to the reclamation of the Amazon Rain Forest [far right].

commitment to human rights, international peace, and environmental survival.

Even his closest friends and colleagues were stunned by the soft-spoken, mild mannered "How" Nissen. His first day in office — May 6th — began at 6:05 a.m., with an executive order pulling all Peace Force troops from poisoned No Man's Lands in Central America, Cuba, Israel, Pakistan, and Indochina, thereby ending over a decade of costly wars and paving the way for America's readmittance to the United Nations.

Those who thought they knew him learned quickly to expect the unexpected. The 150,000 PAX troops pulled from every war-torn corner of the world were not left idle. Nissen dispatched them to Brazil, to seize and surround the dying remains of the great Amazon Rain Forest, forcing U.S. hamburger corporations to cease their destruction of the world's greatest and most precious source of oxygen. The newly-fitted and expanded Environmental Protection Agency followed the troops in, and, despite repeated military attacks by Brazilian nationals and Hamburger-sponsored terrorists, EPA experts have begun the process of reforestation.

It soon became clear to all that the new president had no intention of stripping his office of the enormous power it had accumulated under Rexall's reign. Within the week the tireless Nissen had brought cries for impeachment from the Rexall Republican Congress — and shouts of joy from liberals, environmentalists, feminists, and ethnic lead-

:rs. Telegrams by the thousands have reached he rebuilt White House, cheering him on vith each new bold initiative. A "silent najority" never envisioned by the far Right :as, a mere six months after his inauguration, :anonized Howard Nissen as the saviour of he soul of America.

By early June he authored and successful-y negotiated the US-Soviet Swords Into Plowshares Disarmament Treaty, compelling both nations to point their enormous laser :annons at their own territories in fixed position that can only be changed by a unanimous vote of the United Nations. By uly he ended months of strife at the Aragones Refinery in the Mexican Territory, igning a handwritten treaty that granted the Apache Nation the refinery and its surround-ing land. With the help of lobby groups and enthusiastic letter campaigns by citizens groups, he is well on his way to forcing through Congress a wide range of social and educational programs unheard-of since before the Mexican War.

Should Erwin Rexall ever rise from his bed at Walter Reed, he will be confronted with an America that scarcely resembles that which he ruled like a king.

Howard Johnson Nissen was born in 1965 in Berkeley, California, the son of Wildflower and Primrose Nissen, to whom he refers lovingly as "hopeless hippies". An only child, he attended a variety of grade and high

THEY SAY IF YOU JOIN *PAX* THEY *CLEAR* YOUR *RECORD*.

YOU CAN'T GET *ARRESTED* OR *ANYTHING*.

MOM'S REALLY GOING TO BE PISSED OFF.

IT'S JUST LIKE THEY *PROMISED*.

THEY DON'T ASK ANY *QUESTIONS*.

THEY'RE TOO BUSY GIVING *ORDERS*.

Welcome to Brazil, Peace Officers. We're two minutes from the rain forest, heading into heavy shelling.

YOU'RE JUST A LITTLE *GIRL*--

YAA.

SMALL FOR MY AGE, SQUID. HAND OFF MY LEG.

P-32F

PAX

ORDER WAS TO *JUMP*, WASHINGTON --

CHUTE'S WORKING--IT'S WORKING --

--IT'S W--

NNFF

BRAKA BRAKA BRAK

LIEUTENANT *MORETTI* --SIR--

SPUK SPUK SPUK

--PRIVATE *WASHINGTON* REPORTING FOR DUTY--

THEY'RE *SAUCING* THE MEN UP *FRONT*--STAY *LOW*--GET THESE *TO* THEM--

JUST A *GIRL*,SIR--I'LL DO IT--

OH GOD JESUS

JESUS

SPUK

SPUK SPUK

SPLTT

P.A.X

SKEE

SKEE

# 2010

PERSONAL CORRESPONDANCE
FROM: Sgt. Martha Washington, Amazon Base 6
TO: Mrs. John Washington, 66 Red Grove #44B,
Chicago, IL 60601
DATE: August 22, 2010

Hi, Mom! Bet you're surprised to hear from me!

Right now I'm sitting in the infirmery. Caught some
Special Sauce in the last Big Mac Attack and
suddenly they're treating me great. I didn't get
hurt too bad, but until the burns heal up a little
more I get to stay out of the fighting. They even
let me use the neatest little lap top to write this
letter. It's no bigger than a toaster but it works
fine.

I'm a sargeant now, after only six months. That
means better pay and I don't have to take orders as
much. I guess PAX is pretty happy with me.

Boy, have they kept me running! It just never lets
up here and they're pretty strict about not letting
us write home. Guess they must have their reasons.

Mom, the Rain Forest is beautiful. The mosquitoes
are all over the place and big as your fist and if
they bite you get really swollen up, though, and at
first it was really scary, in the forest. It's
bigger than anything and it's always dark, and
there's more weird animals than in a zoo. They make
tons of noise when the shelling isn't going on, and
they sound as weird as they look. I always thought

tons of noise when the shelling isn't going on, and they sound as weird as they look. I always thought nature was supposed to be quiet like a postcard. When I'm done with work I like to take walks in it. Sometimes I run into the Reforesters but they're okay, and mostly I get to be all by myself. One time I saw a little monkie with eyes so smart you'd swear it was really a human. Half expected it to talk with me and it did click at me like I was supposed to understand. But maybe I was just imagining things.

Anyway, the big news is that I'll be coming home in a few weeks, they say before the end of the year! Commander Bracket said I could practicly count on it even though he says I'm a good soldier and he'll miss me. Maybe I'll even be home for Christmas!

Love to you and John and sorry if the letter sounds queer. Guess I should've studied harder back in school at English.

See you soon I hope!

Martha

--YOU FOUL THIS *UP* AND WE'RE *ALL* DEAD -- *SHH*. HEARD SOMETHING...

--JUST FOLLOW THE *LIGHT*, YOU *ASSHOLES*--

...OH, CHRIST...

LIEUTENANT MORETTI...?

BLAM

AAAAA

BLAM

BLAM

BLAM

BETTER *CONFIRM* THE *KILL* -- IF SHE'S *ALIVE*, I'M *SCREWED*--

NO *TIME*, MORETTI. WE GOT A *FOREST* TO BURN.

FOREST TO BURN

FOREST
TO BURN

MORETTI

LIEUTENANT
MORETTI

MORETTI
LET THEM IN

THEY'LL
BURN IT
ALL

ICEMAN'S
HERE

NO HE
ISN'T

BURN
DOWN MY
FOREST

--OOF--
SHIT I
HATE THIS
PLACE

COME ON
--SET THOSE
INCENDIARIES--

FOREST
TO BURN

--SO
WE CAN
GET THE
HELL--

--OUT--

SHKK

HUK

HUKK
KAFFF

MORETTI
*COUGHS*

SKREKK

AND THE
GROWN UPS

DICKENS

THE GROWN
UPS ALWAYS
COUGH

GET A *MEDICAL*
TEAM. THIS ONE'S
*BREATHING.*

THE *SURGEONS*
COULDN'T LET
YOU DIE. THEY
WORKED DAY
AND *NIGHT.*

YOU'RE
A *HERO.*
YOU SAVED
THE WHOLE
*FOREST.*

WE'VE GOT A SURPRISE FOR YOU.

YOU MAY SEE HER NOW, LIEUTENANT.

THANK YOU, NURSE. I'D LIKE TO BE ALONE WITH HER.

WOULD YOU LOOK AT THIS PIECE OF SHIT *PROSTHETIC* THEY GAVE ME? DAMNED *ANTIQUE*.

DON'T WORRY, THOUGH. MY *FAMILY'S* GOT A *STATE-OF-THE-ART* LUNG ON IT'S WAY. I'LL BE GOOD AS NEW.

MY FAMILY'S GOT A LOT OF MONEY. A LOT OF POWER.

NOBODY'S GOING TO BELIEVE SOME STREET NIGGER OUT OF A NUT HOUSE THAT I'M ANYTHING BUT A WAR HERO.

SO LET'S *BOTH* BE WAR HEROES, WASHINGTON'.

AND DON'T GIVE ME ANY *SHIT*.

I DON'T GIVE HIM ANY SHIT

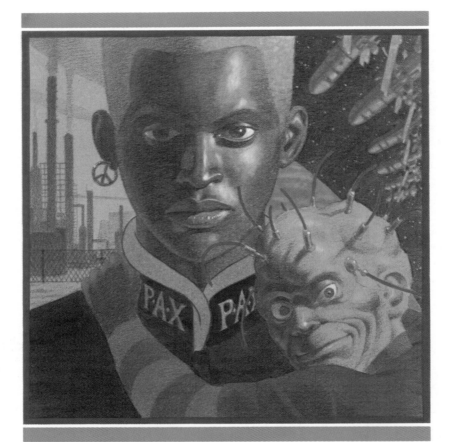

# 2: TRAVEL & ENTERTAINMENT

2008: OUR COUNTRY IS AT WAR WITH FORTY FOREIGN NATIONS-- AND WITH *ITSELF*.

BUDGET CUTS FORCE AUTHORITIES TO SHUT DOWN *PRISONS* AND *MENTAL INSTITUTIONS*, BRINGING HIDEOUS *POVERTY* AND *VIOLENCE* TO CITY STREETS.

PRESIDENT *ERWIN REXALL*, FACING THE THREAT OF HIS FIRST DEFEAT IN FOUR ELECTIONS, DECLARES *MARTIAL LAW*.

CONGRESS GRANTS THE *SURGEON GENERAL* AUTHORITY TO CONDUCT HIS 'WAR ON SICKNESS!'

*CRIME* IS NOT A *DISEASE*.

*DISEASE* IS A *CRIME*.

THE *HEALTH POLICE* JOIN THE *PEACE FORCE* IN THE URBAN PACIFICATION EFFORT.

FOR A TIME THE STREETS ARE SILENT.

THEN COME THE *RIOTS* -- AND THE *BATTLES*. AUTHORITIES ARE FORCED TO SURRENDER ENTIRE *NEIGHBORHOODS* TO MILITANT FACTIONS.

MAY 5, 2009: A *FIREBOMB* REDUCES THE *WHITE HOUSE* TO A BURNT SHELL.

SIXTY-SEVEN SEPARATE REVO- LUTIONARY GROUPS CLAIM RESPONSIBILITY FOR THE ATROCITY.

BADLY BURNED, PRESIDENT REXALL LAPSES INTO A *COMA*. WHO WILL REPLACE HIM?

AMONG THE DEAD: VICE PRESIDENT *CARGO*, ATTORNEY GENERAL *SPHINCTER* AND EVERY MEMBER OF THE REXALL CABINET--

--EXCEPT *HOWARD NISSEN*, ACTING SECRETARY OF AGRICULTURE.

A LIBERAL DEMOCRAT MOMENTARILY BOOSTED INTO THE POSITION BY THE DEATH OF SECRETARY *PLACEBO* THREE DAYS EARLIER.

EVERYONE HAD BEEN SURE THAT HE WOULD SHORTLY BE FIRED.

IT WAS NO SECRET THAT REXALL WAS DISPLEASED WITH HIS MILITANT ENVIRONMENTALISM.

MAY 9, 2009: HOWARD NISSEN IS SWORN IN AS THE FIRST NEW PRESIDENT OF THE UNITED STATES IN THIRTEEN YEARS.

MAY 10, 2009: NISSEN'S FIRST *EXECUTIVE ORDER* WITHDRAWS ALL *PEACE FORCE* TROOPS FROM POISONED NO-MAN'S-LANDS IN EVERY CORNER OF THE EARTH--

--ENDING MORE THAN A DECADE OF COSTLY WARS AND PAVING THE WAY FOR AMERICA'S RE-ADMITTANCE TO THE UNITED NATIONS.

BUT THE 150,000 *PAX* TROOPS ARE NOT LEFT IDLE FOR LONG.

JUNE 1, 2009 PRESIDENT NISSEN ORDERS A FULL-SCALE INVASION OF BRAZIL'S *AMAZON RAIN FOREST*.

*PAX* TROOPS DEFEND WHAT LITTLE REMAINS OF THE FOREST FROM RUTHLESS INTERNATIONAL FAST FOOD CORPORATIONS IN A WAR THAT CONTINUES TO THIS DAY.

JUNE 21, 2009: NISSEN SUCCESS-FULLY NEGOTIATES THE LANDMARK 'SWORDS INTO PLOWSHARES' TREATY--

--*SOVIET* AND *U.S. LASER CANNONS* ARE AIMED AT EACH COUNTRY'S *OWN TERRITORY*.

JUNE 30, 2009: NISSEN'S FIRST CRISIS. A BAND OF *APACHE INDIANS* SEIZE THE OLD *LUNDORF OIL REFINERY* IN THE MEXICAN TERRITORY.

NISSEN'S SOLUTION SHOCKS SOME-- AND THRILLS MANY.

MY FRIENDS, IT'S TIME WE SET THINGS RIGHT.

THE GENOCIDE OF NATIVE AMERICANS MUST STOP.

THE FEDERAL GOVERNMENT HAS PURCHASED THE LUNDORF REFINERY--

--AND OFFERS IT TO THE APACHE PEOPLE AS A GESTURE OF GOODWILL, IN HOPE THAT THEY MAY PROSPER.

MARCH 31, 2010: PRESIDENT NISSEN RECEIVES THE *NOBEL PEACE PRIZE*.

SHOULD ERWIN REXALL EVER RISE FROM HIS BED AT WALTER REED--

HE WILL BE CONFRONTED WITH AN AMERICA THAT SCARCELY RESEMBLES THE NATION HE RULED LIKE A KING.

AND TELL THEM *MORETTI* SENT YOU, BABE.

YOU *KNOW* WE'RE ALL *COUNTING* ON YOU.

...YES, CAPTAIN.

GOT ITS ATTENTION.

ARMING....

POOM
POOM

--INCOMING--

--TAKE *COVER*--

BOOOM

--IN THE *FOURTH* ATTEMPT TO ASSASSINATE PRESIDENT NISSEN THIS WEEK BY THE *ARYAN THRUST.*

THE MILITANT GAY RACIST GROUP HAS SWORN *REVENGE* FOR THE ACCIDENTAL LASER CANNON INCINERATION OF ITS APPALACHIAN MOUNTAIN *STRONGHOLD* ...

...AN ACCIDENT *APPLAUDED* BY THE *SURGEON GENERAL...*

THIS COUNTRY IS *BLIGHTED. POISONED. CANCEROUS.* ITS *MOUNTAINS* ARE SUPPURATING *SORES.* ITS *PEOPLE* ARE MUTATING *BACTERIA* --

-- *LASER SURGERY* IS *EXACTLY* WHAT AMERICA NEEDS.

THE SURGEON GENERAL HAS DISPATCHED *HEALTH POLICE* TO 'DISINFECT' APPALACHIA. NO CASUALTIES HAVE BEEN REPORTED...

SEX SCANDAL *ROCKS* THE VATICAN! AFTER THIS:

SOMETIMES IT JUST GETS TO ME AND I HAVE TO CRY--

--WISH I COULD TALK TO MOM SHE'S NEVER SCARED--

--I WANT MOM AND INSTEAD THIS CAT SHOWS UP.

THIS BIG CAT. A PANTHER...

...FIRST TIME I SEE HER, I ALMOST THROW UP--BUT ALL SHE DOES IS LOOK ME OVER AND WALK AWAY...

GHHAAA

I SAID NO FRATER-NIZATION BETWEEN OFFICERS.

DO WE UNDERSTAND EACH OTHER, GENTLEMEN?

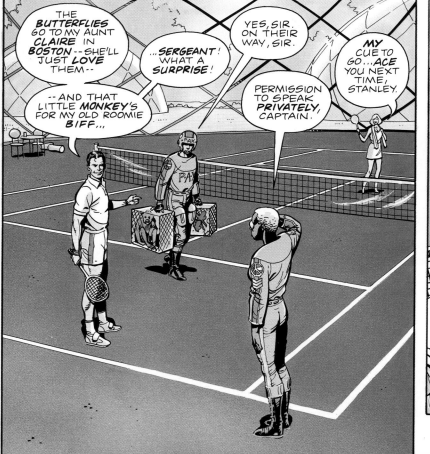

THE BUTTERFLIES GO TO MY AUNT CLAIRE IN BOSTON--SHE'LL JUST LOVE THEM--

--AND THAT LITTLE MONKEY'S FOR MY OLD ROOMIE BIFF...

...SERGEANT! WHAT A SURPRISE!

PERMISSION TO SPEAK PRIVATELY, CAPTAIN.

YES, SIR. ON THEIR WAY, SIR.

MY CUE TO GO...ACE YOU NEXT TIME, STANLEY.

IT'S ABOUT YOUR TRANSFER REQUEST, ISN'T IT, SERGEANT? NO CAN DO. WE NEED YOU RIGHT AT THE FRONT OF THINGS.

YOUR FAULT FOR BEING SUCH A GO-GETTER.

I DON'T MIND THE COMBAT, SIR. IT'S THE MEN.

I'M THE ONLY OFFICER IN SQUAD FOUR WHO DIDN'T COME STRAIGHT FROM DEATH ROW.

GIVING YOU A ROUGH TIME, AREN'T THEY? SORRY, DOLL, BUT YOU'LL JUST HAVE TO BUCK UP.

PERMISSION TO SPEAK... CANDIDLY, SIR.

I'VE KEPT MY MOUTH SHUT. I HAVEN'T TOLD ANYBODY HOW YOU SOLD US OUT.

THWAKK

THAT WILL BE ALL, SERGEANT.

KHAFFF

I WANT TO KILL HIM.

THIS TIME SHE SNIFFS ME.

-- A NEWS TWELVE DATA RAID REVEALS THE LASER CANNON MISFIRE WAS CAUSED BY AN EXPERIMENTAL COMMAND SYSTEM--

--UTILIZING PSYCHIC SCHIZOPHRENICS LITERALLY WIRED IN TO COMPUTER SOFTWARE.

COMING UP: VICTORIOUS PAX TROOPS PRESS THEIR ADVANTAGE --CHARGING THE FATBOY CATTLE-FIELDS AT THE EDGE OF THE AMAZON...

NO **SIGN** OF THEM--THEY'VE PULLED **OUT**--

OH, **JESUS**--THE **COWS**--THEY'RE **RIGGED**!

I'M GOING TO MISS THE FOREST.

THE FIGHTING SUCKED.

BUT I'M GOING TO MISS THE FOREST.

STEP **LIVELY**, SERGEANT.

WE'RE MOVING **OUT**.

WE'RE **ALL** MOVING OUT.

THE WAR'S **OVER**.

THE WAR'S OVER.

IT'S OVER.

HE GIVES MORETTI ANOTHER MEDAL AND ANOTHER **PROMOTION**--TO **COLONEL**.

HE GIVES **ME** ANOTHER **MEDAL**.

HE HAS **SAD EYES**. HE LISTENS REALLY **CLOSELY** WHEN I TALK TO HIM ABOUT THE **GREEN**.

--**CABRINI GREEN**. I WAS **BORN** THERE.

THEY CALL IT A **HOUSING PROJECT** BUT IT'S A **PRISON**...

**HORRIBLE**. MY **GOD**. IF ALL THIS IS **TRUE**...

..., IT WON'T **STAND**. NOT ONE MORE **DAY**.

I **PROMISE** YOU THAT, SERGEANT.

MOM.

I LOVE THE PRESIDENT.

THE NEW ONE, I MEAN.

JUST DON'T **WORRY** MOM--NOT ABOUT **ME**

THEY SAY THERE'S NO **WAY** I HAVE TO LEAVE **HOME**. NOT EVER **AGAIN**.

SEE WHERE WE GOT IT AIMED?

I SAY THE WORD --I WHISPER THE WORD AND WASHINGTON D.C'S A CRATER. SO NO SHIT.

YES I UNDERSTAND.

GIVE ME THAT DAMNED GUN, YOU BITCH.

AND HAND OVER THAT SWORD OR I'LL BREAK YOUR NECK.

I'LL BE TAKING THAT CASE, PECKER-WOOD.

I SAID GIVE ME THAT SWORD.

BROUGHT A DARKIE, DID YOU? WHAT'S YOUR NAME, DARKIE?

YOU KNOW YOU CAN'T FIRE THAT THING. NOT IN HERE.

BULLETS ARE BOUND TO PUNCTURE A WALL. BLOW EVERYTHING OUT.

KILL YOURSELF, SHOOTING THAT THING.

SYSTEMS CRASH ON SHUTTLE *FOUR-OH-NINER* -- SHE'S GOING *DOWN*.

IMPACT. SHE'S DOWN.

WAIT--

HER MAIN ENGINE'S ABOUT TO BLOW-- WASHINGTON'S FINISHED--

WHFF

PAK
PAK

SHE'S OUT OF THE *SHUTTLE*--ON HER *FEET*--

--SHE'S *RUNNING*-- GOT HER *BUCKMINSTER* WITH HER--SHE HAS A *CHANCE*...

*FIRE'S* AT THE *FUEL LINE*-- SHUTTLE'S ABOUT TO *BLOW*--

PAK

PAK

PAK

OH NO. OH GOD--

ALL UNITS. WITHDRAW. NOW. YOU'VE CROSSED THE LINE. THE APACHES--

GET OUT OF THERE-- GET OUT--

DO NOT RETURN FIRE--

OH, SHIT--

PFOOM

--MARTHA GET UP-- NOT IN FOREST. NOT RAINING.

NO TIME FOR FLASHBACK, MARTHA. WAKE UP. PEOPLE COMING.

MORETTI YOU BASTARD

NNFF. WHUH...? PEOPLE...?

MARTHA.

NNFF

NNNNOO--

THWAKK

IT WAS HAILED AS HIS **CROWNING ACHIEVEMENT**...

--THE FEDERAL GOVERNMENT HAS PURCHASED THE LUNDORF REFINERY--

--AND OFFERS IT TO THE APACHE PEOPLE AS A GESTURE OF GOODWILL, IN HOPE THAT THEY MAY PROSPER.

...BUT **THIS** IS THE **LEGACY** PRESIDENT NISSEN HAS BEQUEATHED TO THE APACHE PEOPLE.

**AIR** SO DESPOILED THAT A SINGLE DAY'S EXPOSURE BRINGS A **HACKING COUGH** TO THE HEARTIEST...

...**SKIN** TURNED **GREY** AND **DISEASED**--

--PAINTED **RED** IN SAD PRIDE, EVERY DAY...

--A *PEOPLE* AND A *RACE* DYING SLOWLY OF *LUNG DISEASE.*

MEMOIRS OF AN AMERICAN PRESIDENT.

DECEMBER 7, 2011

EVEN THE MOST *DEVOTED* SUPPORTERS OF PRESIDENT NISSEN LIST THE *APACHE NATION* AMONG HIS MANY *FAILURES*...

IT'S LATE, AND I'M TIRED.

TIRED...

GLUG

...THE WORD HARDLY BEGINS TO DESCRIBE THE BONE-DEEP, SOUL-DEEP FATIGUE...

--SIXTY THOUSAND AMERICAN LIVES LOST IN THE AMAZON WAR--

...THAT LEAVES ME LIKE A DEAD MAN AT THE END OF EVERY SINGLE DAY.

...BUT SOMEHOW I CONTINUE, IN SPITE OF IT ALL...

...I MUST CONTINUE...

--CURRENCY COLLAPSE--

...MUST STAY TRUE TO THE DESTINY THAT HAS SETTLED SO HEAVILY ACROSS...

...HEAVILY UPON MY SHOULDERS--

--SHIT--

--*SHIT* GODDAMNIT...

GLUG

YOU NEVER HAD IT SO BAD.

# Apache Sundown

## Poverty and Despair in the Apache Nation

### by Lisa Nordik

**Nothing to lose:**
*Redfeather's angry army*

**D**ancing Rabbit, four years old, stands over an oil-can filled with a bright-red mixture the texture of creosote. She dips a dirty cloth into the mix and spreads it across her acne-ridden face, her sunken chest, her swollen belly. Soon she is more or less the color of her Apache ancestors. Behind her, lined liked derelicts outside a mission, are the other coughing, grey-skinned women of her tribe.

This sad, strange ritual is repeated every morning by every member of the Apache Nation before they go to their posts at the fifty year old Lundorf Refinery. The refinery is a shameful antique, lacking even the most rudimentary of air-cleansing technology. It coughs purple-black smoke into the once beautiful sky of the Mexican Territory. The eyes sting the moment one arrives. The mouth is filled with an awful, oily taste. A single day's exposure to the

**Lost pride, lost hope:** *An Apache girl paints her skin*

President Nissen's signature added to the treaty last year, the tribe looked forward to cultural and economic independence. But with America's increasing use of solar power, the oil producing nations of the world have faced financial cataclysm, and with them, the lofty dream of Redfeather has turned to oil-black despair.

Starving, but armed to the teeth: A Presidential Decree protects the Apache from any assault from PAX. PAX is, in fact, forbidden even from returning fire from the warlike tribe. Nonetheless, Redfeather has formed a state of the art militia — and observers worry that Redfeather may once

**A desperate, angry Chief:** *On the warpath?*

poisoned air will give even the hardiest of visitors a chronic, gut-wrenching cough. A year's labor at the refinery has inflicted forty per cent of the inhabitants with a variety of undiagnosed, untreated lung diseases. There aren't many of the revered Old Ones left. Most have died coughing blood.

**Redfeather's dream:** The handsome young leader of the Apache Nation stirred hopes nationwide for his people and inspired an outpouring of pickets and protests when he led one hundred warriors to seize the refinery on July 20, 2009. He produced a two hundred year old treaty granting his people the land upon which the refinery was built. With

THEY DON'T *HURT* ME OR RAGGYANN THEY *FEED* US--

--IT'S *SNAKE* MEAT THAT TASTES LIKE *OIL* BUT THEY *FEED* US--

--SLAPPING ME *AROUND* LIKE THEY DID WAS FOR *SHOW.* FOR THE *PEACE FORCE.*

THEY THINK THEY'LL GET *MONEY* FOR ME ...

FEW DAYS ALONG THEY'RE ALL *OVER* ME WITH QUESTIONS ABOUT THEIR *COMPUTERS.*

HAD A *BETTER* SYSTEM AT THE *GREEN.* *THIS* ONE WAS BUILT BEFORE I WAS *BOR, J.* IT'S A *MESS.*

MMMFF

STRONG BODY. BEAUTIFUL IN MOON-LIGHT.

KAFF

NEVER *COUGHED* BEFORE -- NOT IN MY WHOLE *LIFE* --

GOT TO GET *OUT* OF HERE.

NO *NANICS* OR *PARANODES* LUNCH BOX *OUT*.

*SCHIZO-PHRENICS*. HEAR INSIDE.

TIME LIKE *EGG*. HEAR INSIDE.

*LIMBICON* NOT *FLOP* ON *CANNON*.

WIREHEADS LIKE *RAGGYANN* TALK. TO. FROM. INOUTPUT. TALK CAN HEAR WIRE-HEADS.

*NAZI FIRE* NOT *FLOP*. WIREHEADS *AGREE*. WIREHEADS *AGREE* DO *NAZI FIRE*. NO *LUNCH BOX*.

NO *ZIPLOCK*. WIREHEADS NOT *FLOP*.

NGG

NGGNO--

THE SPIN TEAM HAS BEEN WORKING ALL NIGHT, MR. PRESIDENT. YOUR SCRIPT IS READY.

UHNNN... DID SOMETHING HAPPEN...?

FOLLOWING THE MURDER OF VICE PRESIDENT ESTEVEZ BY APACHE TERRORISTS, PRESIDENT NISSEN IMPOSED A NEWS BLACKOUT IN THE MEXICAN TERRITORY...

...AND PROMISED SWIFT, DECISIVE ACTION TO RESOLVE THE APACHE CRISIS.

NISSEN REFUSED TO RULE OUT THE POSSIBILITY OF MILITARY INTERVENTION...

YOU'RE JUST A SIDE ORDER, WASHINGTON. THIS ONE SWEET MOVE OF MINE WILL RUIN THAT STUPID DRUNK OF A PRESIDENT...

...AND MAKE ME THE MOST POWERFUL SON OF A BITCH ON THIS PLANET...

MORETTI...?

...JUST A SIDE ORDER...BUT A DAMN DELICIOUS ONE--

I SWORE YOU'D DIE FOR IT THE SECOND YOU SHOVED THAT BAYONET BETWEEN MY RIBS--

-- AND HERE NISSEN WAS, PRIMING YOU TO BECOME A MEDIA EVENT. "SHE'S PERFECT," HE SAID...

"SHE'S BLACK. GREW UP POOR. WOULD'VE ENDED UP A JUNKIE OR A HOOKER IF IT WEREN'T FOR PAX..."

# 3: HEALTH & WELFARE

DISEASE IS NOT CONFINED TO THE *BODY*. IT IS IN THE *MIND*. IT IS IN THE *SOUL*. AND IT IS *KILLING* THIS COUNTRY.

AMERICA IS *KILLING ITSELF*. WITH *BAD HABITS*. *BAD ATTITUDES* --

-- AND *BAD MUSIC*.

THE SURGEON GENERAL DECLARED THE SOUTHWEST *RADIOACTIVE ZONE* A '*PHYSICAL, MORAL* AND *ESTHETIC BLIGHT*'--

-- *CONDEMNING* THE GROWING POPULARITY OF THE *MUTANT MUSICAL GROUP SEVERE TIRE DAMAGE* --

-- AND REQUESTING *AUTHORITY* TO *STERILIZE* THE RADIOACTIVE ZONE WITH SPACE CANNON *LASER FIRE*.

NOR SHOULD THE *USERS* OF THIS *POISON* TO THE *EAR* AND *PSYCHE* BE SPARED THE WRATH OF THE *HEALTHY*.

PRESIDENT NISSEN REFUSED TO COMMENT ON THIS LATEST DEMAND FOR EXPANSION OF THE *HEALTH ENFORCEMENT DEPARTMENT* --

-- NOR ON WIDE-SPREAD *RUMORS* THAT THE *APACHE NATION'S* TERRORIST ASSASSINATION OF VICE PRESIDENT *ESTEVEZ* WAS ONLY THE *FIRST BLOW* OF A GREATER *WAR*.

WHEN WE RETURN: *CONGRESS* APPROVES A HEALTH ENFORCEMENT CRACKDOWN ON ILLEGAL '*BEEFEASYS*' --

-- WHILE THE OUTLAW *FAT BOY BURGERS* CORPORATION WARNS THAT PROTEST SUICIDES BY BEEF ADDICTS WILL *CONTINUE* UNTIL THE *94TH AMENDMENT* IS *REPEALED* ...

# EXECUTIVE
# ORDER

TO: **GEN. LUCIUS SPANK,** Commander, Joint Chiefs Of Staff

FROM: **THE CHIEF**

February 16, 2011        3:04 A.M.

This order is to be destroyed immediately after you have committed its contents to memory.

Bear in mind that any discussion of this Order with anyone under any circumstances will force me to use Executive Privilege as defined in the 36th Amendment. Your summary court-martial and execution will be the price of disobedience.

You will instruct Peace Force Lt. Colonel Stanford Moretti to deploy laser fire from an orbiting laser cannon to eradicate the Apache Nation from the face of the earth.

You will falsify evidence to the effect that the Apache Nation is readying a nuclear strike on Washington, D.C..

This operation must leave no survivors and will be carried out by sunrise tomorrow morning.

Best to Helena and the kids.

*Nissen*

**PRESIDENT**

--SURPRISE **LASER CANNON ATTACK** INCINERATES THE TERRORIST **APACHE NATION'S** NUCLEAR THREAT TO OUR NATIONAL SECURITY.

THE **SURGEON GENERAL** HAS APPLAUDED THIS LATEST LASER DEPLOYMENT AND DISPATCHED **HEALTH ENFORCEMENT** TROOPS TO COMPLETE THE 'DISINFECTION' PROCESS.

THE NAME OF THE HEROIC **PEACE FORCE** OFFICER KILLED IN THE EXCHANGE HAS BEEN WITHHELD PENDING NOTIFICATION OF THE NEXT OF KIN...

THE RECORD WILL SHOW THAT YOUR DAUGHTER DIED IN THE LINE OF **DUTY**, MRS. WASHINGTON.

SHE WAS DEARLY LOVED AT **PAX**. PLEASE BELIEVE THAT AS HER **COMMANDING OFFICER**...

... HER DEATH IS A **PERSONAL** LOSS TO ME. WE WERE LIKE BROTHER AND SISTER...

TOYOTA

♪

MELTING ICE CAPS MEAN **BIG BUCKS** FOR ENTREPRENEUR **JAMES DWINELL**, WHO INTRODUCED THE **AQUACAB** TO MANHATTAN'S SUBMERGED STREETS.

CRANKY AS EVER, THE CITY'S GONE BACK TO WORK.

IN A RELATED STORY, HEROIC **PEACE FORCE** TROOPS HAVE INTERVENED IN THE MANHATTAN-BROOKLYN **WAR**, NOW IN ITS THIRD WEEK...

...WHILE MANHATTAN BOROUGH PRESIDENT **BELUGA** VOWS THAT THE SHELLING WILL CONTINUE:

HEY, **WE'RE** NOT HURTING. THIS IS A **GREAT** TOWN TO LIVE IN. THE **GREATEST.**

**PRESIDENT NISSEN** TODAY DENIED **CHARGES** THAT PEACE FORCE INVOLVEMENT WILL ONLY **ESCALATE** THE CONFLICT...

GID LOST. YOU DON'T KNOW **SHIT.**

...THE **LATEST** UNPOPULAR MOVE BY THE MAN ONCE KNOWN AS THE 'SAVIOR OF THE SOUL OF AMERICA'...

...WHO NOW FACES A 98% DISAPPROVAL RATE NATIONWIDE.

A NATIONWIDE POLL INDICATES A GROUNDSWELL OF SUPPORT FOR FORMER PRESIDENT **ERWIN REXALL**, STILL COMATOSE AFTER TWO YEARS...

MEATRACK

# YOU CAN LOOK
## –BUT YOU BETTER NOT TOUCH!

**B**illionaire Burt Blank liked his bitches big, brawny and BAD — and that's exactly how he BUILT them! Blank brought BIG BUCKS to bear to breed body-proud BABES. But Blank's GENE GENIUSES grew BALL-BUSTERS instead of perfect parts PARTY GIRLS — tough as titanium and MEAN as a mother-you-know-what! These built-for-battle bimbos went BERSERK when Blank got a bump in his pump — and handed the hapless horny his HEAD — not to mention his own JOHN HENRY! The old wiener-wangler was WET WADS and the few fearsome foxes he financed were fixing for a FALL till some fast operator found a FORTUNE by marketing the malicious maidens into MILITARY MIGHT! Watch the SKIES, pal!

I WAS SURPRISED BY YOUR CALL, MRS. WASHINGTON. I DON'T THINK THIS IS WISE.

HE'S RIGHT, MOMMA. YOU'RE NOT DOING YOURSELF ANY GOOD. THOSE NIGHTMARES YOU'VE BEEN HAVING...

QUIET, JOHN. I WON'T BELIEVE MY BABY'S DEAD UNTIL I SEE HER.

I'M AFRAID THERE ISN'T MUCH TO SEE, MRS. WASHINGTON. THE HEAT WAS INCREDIBLE...

NOW PLEASE. LET'S NOT MAKE THIS ANY WORSE.

COME ON, MOMMA. THIS IS NO GOOD. LET'S GO.

WASHINGTON

IF I HAD MY SAY ABOUT IT, THERE'D BE A THIRTY GUN SALUTE -- A HUNDRED PAX OFFICERS IN FULL DRESS...

...BUT WE'VE HAD SUCH BUDGET CUTS...

IT'S ALL RIGHT, COLONEL. WE'D LIKE TO BE ALONE WITH HER. IF YOU DON'T MIND.

YOU WON'T ARGUE WITH ME ABOUT IT ANYMORE, JOHN. MY BABY ISN'T DEAD. I'D KNOW IT IF MY BABY WAS DEAD. THEY SHOWED US NOTHING BUT A BURNT SKELETON THAT COULD'VE BEEN ANYBODY AND IT WASN'T MARTHA.

YES, MOMMA.

I DON'T KNOW WHY THEY'RE DOING THIS BUT IT'S NOT LIKE IT WAS WITH KEN I KNEW HE WAS DEAD BEFORE THEY EVEN TOLD US IT'S NOT LIKE IT WAS WITH KEN MARTHA'S ALIVE AND SHE'LL FIND A WAY TO LET US KNOW SO WE'LL GO HOME AND WAIT FOR HER.

YES, MOMMA.

MARTHA WASHINGTON 1995-2011

I'D CONSIDER IT A PERSONAL FAVOR IF YOU'D KEEP WASHINGTON'S NAME OUT OF THE MEDIA, BIFF.

SHE'D HAVE WANTED IT THAT WAY.

DON'T WORRY, MARGARET. EVERYTHING WILL BE ALL RIGHT.

WILL YOU LOOK AT THE *TIME*! YOU'RE DUE IN *GROUP THERAPY*.

NO ...NOT *GROUP*...

MARTHA WASHINGTON...

COCHISE. RECORD.

YES, SIR. RECORDING.

BABY'S BREATH WASSERSTEIN, PERSONAL NOTES APRIL FIFTH, 2011. THE APACHE NATION IS DEAD.

BUT THIS IS NO TIME FOR *SENTIMENT*...

EIGHTY PER CENT OF THE APACHE PEOPLE SUFFERED FROM *LUNG DISEASE* AND *SKIN CANCER*.

THE *DRUGS* WERE GREAT, BUT THE *APACHE NATION* JUST WASN'T A VERY GOOD IDEA TO *BEGIN* WITH.

EVEN SO, I HAVE TO FIND OUT *WHO* WAS BEHIND THIS. AND *WHY*. MAYBE I'M BEING *SENTIMENTAL* AFTER ALL...

...OR MAYBE I'M JUST TRYING TO AVOID GOING BACK TO *DAD'S* UTTERLY BORING BUSINESS.

COCHISE. THE *CAVE*. LOSE IT.

WHOOF!

YES, SIR.

ALWAYS *OVER-DOING* IT, COCHISE. GET THE *CAR*.

YES, SIR. I'M SORRY ABOUT OVER-DOING IT, SIR.

NOT *DADJOB*.

NOT *APACHE* FASHION. MARTHA. ZIPLOCK.

MARTHA. STUCK IN HEAD. ZIPLOCK. STUCK IN HEAD.

IT'S TRUE. I CAN'T GET HER OUT OF MY MIND...

NEED *RAGGYANN*. MARTHA'S *BEST* FRIEND. NO LUNCH.

THIS *ISN'T* MY *PLACE.* THIS *ISN'T* MY *STUFF.*

SNOWDEN

YOU HAVEN'T EVEN *TOUCHED* YOUR *DINNER*, MARGARET. NEED HELP GETTING IT *OPEN*?

YOU KNOW YOU HAVE TO KEEP YOUR *STRENGTH* UP, MARGARET.

NO. THERE'S DRUGS IN THE FOOD. I DON'T WANT NO MORE DRUGS.

THERE'S A LOT MORE DRUGS IN *THIS*, MARGARET.

THAT'S NOT MY NAME.

YOU LITTLE *TWAT*. DO YOU *KNOW* WHAT YOU'RE *DOING* TO ME?

SHE *TALKS* SO I KNOW WHERE SHE *IS*.

SOMETHING *HEAVY* FALLS RIGHT INTO MY *HAND*.

HUKK

FIST LIKE A *HAMMER* IN MY STOMACH--*RIB* BREAKS--

IF I COULD *SEE* HER I COULD *FIGHT* HER--

JUST LIKE YOU *WANT*-- NO MORE *DRUGS*--NOT *TODAY*--

NO *DRUGS*-- YOU'LL FEEL EVERY *SECOND* OF THIS YOU *TWAT*--

OPEN DOOR.

YES, SIR!

SNOWDEN

--*DOOR HISSES*. HAZEL BREATHES IN. SCARED.

SIR-- I'M *SORRY*, SIR.

HUK HHUU*UKK*K

BLOOD EXCHANGED. BAD.

SNAK

MM GMM PHAAA AAA

CRUNCHH

SHKKK

AAAA AAHH HGG.

BAD NURSE.

BAD CLONE.

THIS **WASHINGTON** -- SHE'S A **DIFFICULT** SUBJECT, SIR.

**SNOWDEN.** MARGARET SNOWDEN. HER NAME. **MARGARET SNOWDEN.** WORLD MUST BELIEVE THAT HER NAME. THEN SHE WILL.

PRETTY NAME. SHE LIKES IT.

AND WHAT DO YOU **WANT**, MR. CHAPLIN?

**CLEAN!** I WANT TO BE **CLEAN!**

NO MORE BAD HABITS. NO MORE BAD HABITS.

**IMPORTANT** PATIENT. MANY SECRETS. MANY SKILLS. AM PAYING SPECIAL ATTENTION. IS GETTING SPECIAL ATTENTION.

YES, SIR. I DON'T MEAN TO MAKE **EXCUSES**, BUT HER **RESISTANCE** IS **AMAZING.** RIGHT OFF THE **CHARTS.**

WE HAVEN'T BEEN ABLE TO BREAK **THROUGH.** THERE HAS YET TO EMERGE A SINGLE **ARCHE-TYPE.** NOT EVEN A HIDDEN **MEMORY.**

I CAN'T **BELIEVE** THIS!

IT'S **REALITY** THERAPY, MR. NEWCOMB--

--**TOUCH** YOURSELF WHERE YOU **SHOULDN'T** AND THIS IS WHAT **HAPPENS.** IT'S FOR YOUR OWN **GOOD.**

I CAN'T **BELIEVE** YOU **DID** THIS... I COULD **KILL** YOU.

**AMPUTATE** LEFT HAND. NO ANESTHETIC.

YES, SIR. RIGHT AWAY, SIR.

I CAN'T BELIEVE I'M **PAYING** FOR THIS.

SNOWDEN HAS **DISCIPLINED** MIND. STRONG MIND. SPECIAL MEASURES REQUIRED. PREPARE **BRAINFEED.**

YES, SIR... CAN I **WATCH**?

NO. TOO PERSONAL.

MUSIC STARTS AGAIN. I DON'T LIKE IT. I REALLY HATE IT.

EVERY *TIME* IT'S *WORSE*. EVERY *TIME* HE DIGS *DEEPER*.

I CAN'T *REMEMBER* MY *NAME*.

ALL THAT'S LEFT ARE LITTLE *PIECES*.

HE PULLS THEM *OUT* OF ME.

HE MAKES THEM *HURT* UNTIL THEY GO *AWAY*.

A *HAND* ON MY *BREAST*.

IT'S SNOWING AND THERE'S A *HAND* ON MY *BREAST*.

MY *NIPPLE* IS REALLY *HARD* AND I'M *SCARED*.

I TELL THE BOY *NO*.

THEN THE *MUSIC* MAKES ME *HURT*.

IT GOES *AWAY*.

THEN HE MAKES ME SO *HAPPY* I *CRY*.

I *HATE* HIM.

I *HATE* HIS *MUSIC*.

I CAN'T *REMEMBER* MY MOM'S *NAME*.

FOR THE LONGEST TIME I *FLOAT* AND IT'S REALLY SCARY. THEN VOICES START *TALKING* TO ME. *NICE* VOICES.

EVEN THOUGH I CAN'T *FEEL* IT THEY'RE GIVING ME NEW *EYES*. I'LL BE ABLE TO *SEE*.

AND THEY'RE *TELLING* ME WHO I *AM* AND THE *MEMORIES* ARE RUSHING IN AND I *KNOW* WHO I AM ...

THE NEW PERSONALITY IS *TAKING*, SIR. SHE SEEMS TO *WELCOME* IT.

CONGRAT-ULATIONS, SIR. I BELIEVE THIS IS A *FIRST*.

FIRST. ONLY USED ON ROBOTS BEFORE. COLLATE MILITARY SECRETS FROM WASHINGTON MEMORY. PREPARE SNOWDEN FOR DUTY.

SMALLEST I **GOT**, SON-- AND IT'S ALL **YOURS**.

AND **HOLD** MY **CALLS**, COULD YOU? JET LAG. THAT **BED** IS CALLING MY **NAME**.

YES, GENERAL SPANK. THANK YOU, GENERAL SPANK. I HOPE YOU ENJOY YOUR STAY WITH US.

KLAK KIKLAKK

PFAMM

EXECUTIVE ORDER

KLAK KIKLAKK

# ThisWeek

December 14, 2011

A General's guilt revealed
# EXECUTIVE ORDER : GENOCIDE

LADIES AND GENTLEMEN, THE PRESIDENT OF THE UNITED STATES.

THE *MEDIA* IS *LYING* TO YOU, MY FRIENDS. THEY *FORGED* THAT BULLSH-- THAT ALLEGED *EXECUTIVE ORDER*...

UHHNNGGG... OH, HELL...

GHHA*AAKK* ...OH *SHIT*...

HHU*UUKKK*    *GGGHUKKK*

OVERCOME BY SUDDEN *NAUSEA*, PRESIDENT NISSEN WAS UNABLE TO RESPOND TO EXPERT TESTIMONY--

--PROVING THAT THE *SIGNATURE* ON THE SO-CALLED '*GENOCIDE ORDER*' WAS UNMISTAKEABLY *HIS*...

*Nissen*

**PRESIDENT**

...EVEN AS A BIPARTISAN *CONGRESSIONAL VOTE* BEGAN THE PROCESS OF *IMPEACHMENT*...

...WHILE *PAX* TROOPS ARE HARD PRESSED TO DEFEND A *WHITE HOUSE* UNDER *SIEGE*.

STRANGELY, FEW OF THE RIOTING CITIZENS HAVE EVEN *HEARD* OF THE *APACHE NATION* ATROCITY WHICH LEFT TWO HUNDRED *INNOCENTS* AND A RACE DEAD...

IT IS AS IF THE INITIAL *PROTESTS* WERE THE *SPARK* TO IGNITE A NATIONAL *FURY*.

FUCK *THIS*.

*RUMORS* FLY --THAT A FULL *THIRD* OF THE *PAX* OFFICERS HAVE *WALKED* OFF THE *JOB*--

--AND THAT *PRESIDENT NISSEN* IS AT THIS MOMENT HOLDING A *SPECIAL MEETING* OF THE *CABINET* TO DISCUSS THE TERMS OF HIS *RESIGNATION*...

WE ARE AS YET UNABLE TO CONFIRM REPORTS THAT **PRESIDENT NISSEN** AND HIS ENTIRE **CABINET** HAVE BEEN KILLED.

THIS MARKS A BIZARRE AND HORRIBLE CASE OF HISTORY REPEATING ITSELF--

--BRINGING TO MIND THE **TERRORIST ATTACK** THAT LEFT **PRESIDENT REXALL** IN A COMA TWO YEARS AGO.

**NUKE** DEEP. NO **LUNCH**.

**QUIET**, RAGGYANN.

WE SHOULD BE GETTING **CLOSE**, COCHISE.

THREE HUNDRED YARDS TO SECURITY PERIMETER. I READ A **COPTER** COMING, SIR. BETTER FIND **COVER**.

BOTTLEBRAIN. **EGG** BEATER-BOTTLEBRAIN

**QUIET**, RAGGYANN.

HERE WE **ARE**, SWEETIE. **FORTRESS HEALTH**. THEY'LL FIX YOU UP **GOOD** HERE.

WHATEVER YOU SAY, BLOSSOM. I GUESS I JUST FEEL A LITTLE SORRY FOR MY **OLD** DOCTORS...

...I'M SURE THEY COULD USE THE **WORK** AND THEY WERE REAL **NICE**...

SNAKK

SNAKK

ANY **SENSE** OF HER, RAGGYANN?

NO MARTHA.

NO, NATHAN, EVERYTHING'S **GREAT**. I JUST **MISSED** YOU, THAT'S ALL.

NATHAN'S MY **BOYFRIEND**. STATIONED IN **APPALACHIA**.

WE'RE **ENGAGED**. WE'RE GOING TO GET **MARRIED**.

IT'S SO GREAT TO HEAR YOUR **VOICE**, HONEY. I'M COUNTING THE **DAYS**, YOU KNOW. TILL WE CAN BE **TOGETHER** ALL THE **TIME**.

ACTUALLY, I TOOK **THREE** SHOWERS. SILLY, HUH? ALL I'M **WEARING** IS A **TOWEL**...

TELL ME --WHAT ARE YOU **DOING**, RIGHT NOW? WHAT EXACTLY?

IT'S MY DAY **OFF** BUT ALL I FELT LIKE DOING WAS TAKING A **SHOWER** AND TALKING TO **YOU**.

...TAKE IT OFF.

WHAT...?

TAKE IT OFF, MARGARET. THE **TOWEL**. I WANT TO IMAGINE WHAT YOU LOOK LIKE.

MARGARET...? I DIDN'T **OFFEND** YOU, DID I?

NO, DARLING. I'M TAKING THE TOWEL OFF **NOW**. THERE. IT'S RIGHT AT MY **FEET**...

WHAT THE HELL...

WHOOM

COCHISE...

I KNOW, SIR. OVER-DOING IT AGAIN. I'M SORRY, SIR.

NO MARTHA HERE. NO MARTHA.

ALL THIS WAY FOR NOTHING.

MARTHA. MARTHAFILE. REAL BIG. NO LUNCH.

CAPTURE IT. FAST.

NOT MARTHA.

KBLAMM

FFT FFT FFT

FFT

FFT FFT

KBLAMM

INTRUDER NEUTRALIZED. DISPATCH CLEAN-UP CREW TO LEVEL THIRTY. DATA CONSOLE.

Yes, Sergeant.

UPLOAD.

**Washington. Jefferson. Lincoln. Roosevelt. Quayle. Rexall. These are names eternally etched in the heart of every true American.**

**But our hearts are proving more durable than our mountains. Acid rain. Gulf stream fallout. You've heard the terms. You know what's happening to this most precious monument. It's up to you to eat a little less. To work a little harder. To live a little cheaper. To go a little further into debt. So you can give. No contribution is too small. Help us save our Legacy. Help us save Mount Rushmore.**

# 4: DEATH & TAXES

THIS IS HOW FAR I'M WILLING TO GO--ANYBODY TRIES TO GET ME AWAY FROM THIS DESK OR CUT ME OFF--

--AND I'M BLOWING MY OWN BRAINS OUT.

I HATE IT WHEN THINGS DON'T MAKE SENSE AND RIGHT NOW THEY DON'T MAKE SENSE.

SUFFERING AN APPARENT NERVOUS BREAKDOWN--

--FORMER ANCHORWOMAN LONI HIROHITO HAS SEIZED CONTROL OF OUR BURBANK STUDIOS.

YOU SHUT UP. THIS IS MY SHOW.

BLAM BLAM

HUK HUK HUK

FOR GOD'S SAKE NOBODY INTERRUPT HER!

JUST YESTERDAY-- JUST YESTERDAY-- THINGS MADE SENSE...

THEY WERE WEIRD BUT THINGS MADE SENSE.

THEN TODAY I GET FIRED AND MY HUSBAND LEAVES ME AND THE PRESIDENT DIES AND SOME TWIT LIEUTENANT COLONEL TAKES OVER AND AMERICA IS HAVING A CIVIL WAR.

HUK HUK

JUST DOESN'T MAKE SENSE ... SOB ...

LONI--DON'T--

BLAMM

HISTORY AS IT HAPPENS--THIS IS AMERICA ON THE MOVE!

MAY 5, 2009: A TERRORIST FIREBOMB ROBS AMERICA OF THE MOST POPULAR PRESIDENT IN OUR COUNTRY'S HISTORY.

BUT ERWIN REXALL, CALLED BY MANY 'THE MAN WHO GAVE AMERICA ITS BALLS BACK'--

--DOES NOT DIE WITH THE REST OF HIS CABINET.

HIS BRAIN IS ALIVE.

WHILE ONLY **ONE** CABINET MEMBER SURVIVES TO TAKE HIS **PLACE**: ACTING SECRETARY OF AGRICULTURE **HOWARD NISSEN**--

--A **DRUNKEN EMBARRASS- MENT** OF THE PRESIDENCY.

GID LOST. YOU DON KNOW **SHIT.**

THEN COMES THE DAY THAT **EVERY- THING** CHANGES.

DECEMBER 19, 2011: **CONGRESS** IS CALLING FOR NISSEN'S **IMPEACHMENT**--

--WHEN, ONCE AGAIN, THE WHITE HOUSE **BLOWS UP.**

**WHO** PLANTED THE BOMB?

HECK, IT COULD'VE BEEN **ANYBODY.** I MEAN, WHO **DIDN'T** WANT NISSEN GONE?

MORETTI MOVES SWIFTLY, DECISIVELY, ESTABLISHING **MARTIAL LAW**...

...UNTIL FREE ELECTIONS CAN BE HELD.

BUT IT IS AS IF AN EMOTIONAL **DAM** HAS BURST.

WITHIN **HOURS** OF NISSEN'S **ASSASSINATION, SECESSION FEVER** SWEEPS THE LAND.

MILITANT FEMINISTS PROVIDED THIS FOOTAGE, INDICATING THAT THEY HAVE SEIZED POWER OVER THE AMERICAN SOUTHEAST --

--DECLARING IT THE **FIRST SEX CONFEDERACY.**

THE VERY **BIRTH-PLACE** OF THE UNION --**NEW ENGLAND**--

--DEMANDS UNITED NATIONS REPRESENTATION AS AN **INDEPENDENT FEDERATION**.

MANHATTAN BOROUGH PRESIDENT **BELUGA** DECLARES **VICTORY** OVER **BROOKLYN**--

--ANNEXING IT AND FORMING THE **EAST COAST CAPITALIST DICTATORSHIP**.

BELUGA **DENIES** THE WIDESPREAD BELIEF THAT HE FACES AS MANY AS FORTY WARRING SEPERATIST MOVEMENTS WITHIN MANHATTAN.

THERE ARE SCATTERED REPORTS OF **SHELLING** ON THE BORDER OF THE **MEXICAN TERRITORY**--

-- AND THE SELF-PROCLAIMED **LONE STAR REPUBLIC**.

WHILE THE **SURGEON GENERAL**, IN NEGOTIATION FOR THE SOVEREIGNTY OF THE PACIFIC NORTHWEST AS A DISEASE-FREE 'GOD'S COUNTRY'--

--MAKES THE MOST STARTLING REVELATION OF ALL:

HE HOLDS THE **LIVING BRAIN** OF **ERWIN REXALL** --WHO CLAIMS THAT HE IS **STILL** IN OFFICE.

HEH... I DON'T REMEMBER **RESIGNING**, BY GOLLY...

WE ARE **CLONING** THE PRESIDENT A NEW **BODY**. IT WILL BE VERY CLEAN.

GOD'S ✚ COUN

IRONICALLY, IT WAS REXALL HIMSELF WHO DRAFTED THE '**NO HOLDS BARRED**' AMENDMENT--

--COMMITTING **MILITARY FORCE** AGAINST ANY ENEMY WHO HOLDS AN AMERICAN CITIZEN **HOSTAGE** ...

I'VE GOT A WHOLE LOT OF WORK TO DO.

I'VE GOT TO SAVE THE *PRESIDENT*-- SAVE A CREW OF *EIGHTY* ON A *SPACE CANNON*

--AND SAVE *RAGGYANN* AND THAT BIG *INDIAN* GUY.

RAGGYANN'S *PSYCHIC*...

SIDEKICK.

MARTHA MARTHA *TALK-THINK*.

WHAT'S YOUR *STATUS*? HAVE THEY PLUGGED YOU IN?

MOVE IT-- COME ON-- MOVE IT--

Repeat. This is not a drill. All hands to Battle Stations. Prepare to lay in defense grid.

WE'RE IN *TROUBLE*, COLONEL. WE'RE STILL *TEN* MINUTES FROM *DEPLOY-MENT*--

--AND I'M READING *INCOMING*. FORTY-EIGHT TACTICALS. APPROACH PATTERN *VARIABLE*.

Reflectors in position. Initiating Grid One.

WE'RE LAYING IN THE *GRID* BUT YOU KNOW HOW IT *IS*--THE ONE THING THESE CANNONS WERE *BUILT* TO DO AND THEY'VE BEEN *HIT* BY EVERY NUKE *THROWN* AT THEM...

COLONEL--IT'S *EL PASO* AGAIN --OUR MEN ARE *SURROUNDED*--

CAN'T YOU SEE I'M *BUSY*?

...GRID TWO IN PLACE. INITIATING GRID THREE.

STUPID, MORETTI. AM STILL ABLE TO SPARE CANNON. AM WILLING TO NEGOTIATE.

YOU'RE COMMITTING AN *ACT OF WAR*, YOU CRAZY OLD FART! YOU'LL *BURN* FOR THIS.

COLONEL-- IT'S *TAMPA*--

DON'T TRY IT. HE'S NOT FEELING RECEPTIVE.

WON'T BURN FROM CANNON. MISSILES WILL HIT. GRID A JOKE.

TWO MINUTES, MORETTI. STUPID.

SIR, I MUST *INSIST*--I'VE FINALLY GOT *RHODE ISLAND* ON THE LINE--

SECURITY! I WANT THIS MAN *SHOT!*

MY NAME'S WASHINGTON

RAGGYANN! THE MISSILES! NOW!

AARGG

KBLAMM CHKCHAKK KBLAMM

NO ZIPLOCK.

THIS IS THE CAPTAIN. THE GRID HAS FAILED. MAKE YOUR PEACE WITH GOD.

CAPTAIN-- I'M READING A *BUILDUP* IN ONE OF THE *NUKES*--TO *PREMATURE DETONATION*--

WHAT DID YOU-- *OOF!*

BOOM

BOOM

FILTHY.

NO RESPONSE...

Pilot access denied pending voice-print identification.

FULL POWER. MAXIMUM ACCELERATION.

FILTHY GIRL. BAD GIRL, SNOWDEN.

Voice identification verified. engaging thrusters.

Cloak engaged. Craft now radar-invisible.

FILTHY.

IT'S ABOUT **TIME** YOU REPORTED, CAPTAIN.

MY **TIME** JUST HAPPENS TO BE **WORTH** SOMETHING.

YES, SIR. I'M SORRY FOR THE DELAY, SIR. THEY PUT UP QUITE A FIGHT. BUT I'M HAPPY TO REPORT THAT FORTRESS HEALTH HAS **FALLEN.** WE HAVE TAKEN COMMAND.

NO SIGN OF THE **SURGEON GENERAL** -- AND, SIR--

--THE PRESIDENT'S BRAIN IS MISSING.

### GOD'S COUNTRY:

The coalition government formed by the Surgeon General and leaders of the New Calvinist Initiative pledges to "lay waste to the impure" and create a smoke-free, drug-free paradise." Prohibited under penalty of death: "bad music, bad food, bad language, contraception, pornography, and adultery." 50,000 battle-hardened Health Enforcement Troops and Pacific Northwest nuclear missile silos provide a formidable military capability.

### WONDERLAND:

The world's largest entertainment complex, it used to be the nation's playground. But funny animal robots are on the warpath demanding "cultural autonomy" and an "end to the enslavement of artificial intelligence." Rumors of mass murder and subjugation of humans remain unconfirmed. Should PAX assault Wonderland, a hostage crisis of unheard-of proportions is a likely scenario. Implementation of the "No holds Barred" Amendment could result in the death of millions.

### REAL AMERICA:

Fat Boy Burger troops surround multimillion-acre cattlefields, breeding, slaughtering and selling to beef-hungry clients in flagrant defiance of the 94th Amendment. The outlaw fast food conglomerate is well-equipped to defend its territory: its million man army and formidable air force were almost a match for PAX in the Amazon War.

# A NATION

**UNITED ST**

### THE MEXICAN TERRITORY:

Still technically United States property, this overpopulated land openly trades with Real America and is Fat Boy's chief source of inexpensive labor. Satellite photos reveal hundreds of illegal cattle-fields, so many that analysts have stopped calling the territory "America's Ireland"; now it's "Burger Heaven." Anti-American sentiment is high, and Mexican-born PAX officers are joining the Fat Boy army in droves. An alliance between the two powers would present an unspeakable threat to the U.S. sovereignty over North America.

# DIVIDED

**AMERICA**

## THE NEW ENGLAND FEDERATION OF STATES:

Militarily weak, this is the most pacifistic of the new governments, and the most likely to seek reunification with the U.S. Sticking point: the Federation seeks to repeal nearly every Constitutional Amendment passed since 1990. And those Green Mountain eggheads who engineered the schiz-out of the IRS Database in 2009 are bound to be up to more mischief than ever.

## THE EAST COAST CAPITALIST DICTATORSHIP

Manhattan strongman Edward Beluga represents no major threat at present to U.S. security. Though strong in conventional forces, Beluga commands no nuclear, chemical or biological capability as yet. Besides, he has his hands full: his troops, weary from the year long Manhattan-Brooklyn War are now fighting block by block against the white gay racist Aryan Thrust, the Black Supremacy Front, and as many as fifty other separatist movements.

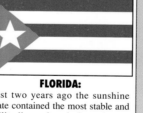

## FLORIDA:

Just two years ago the sunshine state contained the most stable and militarily equipped planned communities in the country. Now its food supply and communication lines have been cut, and its annexation by Cuba seems inevitable.

## THE FIRST SEX CONFEDERACY:

Former First Lady Amanda Nissen, declaring that "everything wrong in the world has been caused by men," emerged as leader in the powerful Southeast Women's Movement, uniting its warring factions to overthrow the governments of the Old South. In her first address, she hit an encouraging note, assuring the U.S. that the Confederacy will seek diplomatic relationships and free trade. The South's abundant farmlands offer a crucial supply of food. Borders remain closed at present to male U.S. citizens. Nissen ordered bans on pornography, marriage, sexist remarks, and "negative role models" in entertainment. Missile silos in the area are abundant but in poor repair. However, a single orbiting laser cannon now answers directly to Nissen, discouraging invasion by PAX.

## THE LONE STAR REPUBLIC:

Texas holds fast to its borders—and to its habits. With a platform of "Guns, beef, and beer" Dallas dentist Billy Bob Coolant established a government based on "community standards," rejecting the First, Fifth, and 94th Amendments out of hand. Their warm and co-dependant relationship with Fat Boy Burgers leaves little room for doubt whose side they would stand on if war breaks out between Fat Boy and PAX. Only Texan hatred of Fat Boy porn movies and continuing border skirmishes with the Mexican Territory prevent a full-fledged alliance. Texas commands a 300,000 man army and possesses first-strike nuclear capability on every city in the western hemisphere. The next American president will have to weigh carefully Texan displeasure with the U.S. Constitution as written.

ON THE WAY *SOUTH* I ASK THE BIG *INDIAN* WHAT HIS *NAME* IS.

HE SAYS IT'S *WASSERSTEIN.*

I TELL HIM THAT DOESN'T SOUND VERY *APACHE.*

HE *LAUGHS* AND SAYS *MY* NAME DOESN'T SOUND VERY *AFRICAN.*

Retros firing. Readying hydrofoil.

HAVEN'T SEEN THE *FOREST* SINCE THE *WAR.* THOUGHT I'D *NEVER* GET TO SEE IT AGAIN.

THE *REFORESTERS* ARE DOING A *GREAT* JOB. IT'S GOING TO BE AS BIG AS IT *EVER* WAS.

AND EVERY-BODY SAYS *NISSEN* WAS A *BAD* PRESIDENT.

HE WAS *RIGHT* ABOUT THE FOREST.

Distress signal engaged. Frequency 444.

WHAT THE **HELL**....?

OH, DEAR. OH MY WORD. I'LL GET A **COLD** AND YOU'LL GO ALL **RUSTY**...

NOW I'M SURE THOSE NICE BOYS THAT BUILT THIS MADE ME **WATER PROOF**, HONEY.

YOU'VE GOT TO LEARN TO **DEPEND** ON PEOPLE. THAT'S WHAT THEY'RE **THERE** FOR.

..., I SAID, **ARE YOU CRAZY**? YOU'RE LETTING THEM **KNOW** WHERE WE ARE!

**MARTHA** NOT **FLOP**, TOMHAWK. NO **LUNCH BOX**.

BY NOW, **PAX** HAS THE SIGNAL AND THEY'VE PASSED IT ALONG TO MORETTI.

MY GUESS IS WE'VE GOT A FEW HOURS TILL HE GETS HERE.

**MORETTI**? LIEUTENANT COLONEL **MORETTI**? THE **WAR HERO**?

THE **TRAITOR**. HE HAS TO KILL THE **PRESIDENT** TO STAY IN **POWER**--AND HE'LL DO ANYTHING HE **CAN** TO KILL **ME**.

THAT'S WHY I BROUGHT US **HERE**--

--THIS **FOREST** IS PROTECTED BY AN **EXECUTIVE ORDER**. MORETTI WON'T BE ABLE TO USE **BOMBS** OR A **LASER CANNON**--THE WAY HE DID ON YOUR **TRIBE**.

HE WAS JUST TRYING TO GET AT ME. I'M REALLY SORRY.

WE'LL CAMP HERE. WE'LL NEED A FIRE...

NOW LET'S SEE WHAT THE **SURGEON GENERAL** CALLS A **FIRST AID KIT.**

HOLY...

YA **CHOO**

CATCH MY **DEATH** OF COLD.

WE'LL JUST HAVE TO **SNUGGLE** ...HEH...

FIRST AID

OUR ODDS JUST GOT **BETTER.**

LET'S CATCH US SOME **FROGS.**

FROGS?

YOU'VE GOT TO BE **CAREFUL** NOT TO **HURT** THE FROGS.

THE NATIVES HERE **WORSHIP** THEM AND YOU'VE GOT TO **RESPECT** THAT SORT OF THING.

THEIR **SKIN** MAKES **POISON.**

THE **NATIVES** USE IT ON THEIR **ARROWS.**

Z

MY BET IS MORETTI WILL PUT TOGETHER A **DEATH SQUAD** -- MAYBE A **DOZEN** MEN. THE KIND WHO'LL KEEP THEIR **MOUTHS** SHUT.

HE'LL PROBABLY GET THEM FROM **SQUAD FOUR...**

SQUAD FOUR...? IS THAT PART OF THE **PEACE FORCE?**

IT **WAS**. PROBABLY STILL IS. **PAX** GAVE AMNESTY TO CONVICTED **MURDERERS** AND PUT THEM IN SQUAD FOUR DURING THE **WAR**.

MORETTI MADE A LOT OF USE OF THEM. EVEN TRIED TO **KILL** ME WITH THEM, ONCE.

LET ME HELP YOU WITH THAT SHOULDER. I'M GOOD WITH MUSCLES.

MORETTI'S REALLY GOT IT **IN** FOR YOU, DOESN'T HE?

YES. I STABBED HIM ONCE. HE WAS TRYING TO BURN DOWN THE **FOREST**. HE TOOK A **BRIBE** FROM THE **FAT BOYS**.

THAT FEELS REALLY GOOD...YOU KNOW, YOU DON'T HAVE TO BE A **PART** OF THIS.

HEY, YOU'RE THE ONE WHO TOLD ME HE KILLED MY **TRIBE**.

BESIDES--

BESIDES, I'VE GOT A CRUSH ON YOU.

--BESIDES, THIS ISN'T AS **BORING** AS GOING BACK TO DAD'S **BUSINESS**.

YOU HUNGRY? I COULD CATCH US SOME-THING.

NO, THANKS. IF WE EAT WE'LL GET SLEEPY.

IF WE SURVIVE THIS, I THINK MAYBE I'D LIKE US TO GET TO KNOW EACH OTHER...

NO. THAT SOUNDS REALLY STUPID. THINK OF SOMETHING BETTER.

DAMN IT-- THAT CRAZY LITTLE **BRAT** IS MAKING AN **ASS** OUT OF ME!

WE BETTER GET STARTED ON THOSE **TRAPS**.

Attention. This vehicle is at self-destruct alert. Detonation in three seconds pending voice identification.

OH, SHIT--

AKABRAKABRAKABRAKABI

OH NO.

NO.

SNAPP

BRAKABI

BRAKABR

FIVE.

SIX.

WE'RE DOING **GREAT**.

BRAKK

SEVEN.

BRAKK

THKK

SEVEN. THAT LEAVES FIVE. AND MORETTI.

*THERE--I GOT THE SIGNAL --REXALL IS A HALF MILE NORTHEAST-- LET'S GO--*

NO. NOT YET. WE'VE GOT TO CONFIRM THE KILLS.

WE *HIT* THEM *BOTH*, MORETTI. LET THE *JUNGLE* DO THE REST.

WASHINGTON *CAN'T* BE LEFT *ALIVE*. THERE *CAN'T* BE ANY *DOUBT*.

YOU'RE *HUNG UP* ON THAT SNATCH, MORETTI. IT'S THROWING YOUR *JUDGEMENT* OFF--

--HEY...

ARE YOU CHALLENGING MY AUTHORITY?

NO, SIR. FOR THE RECORD, I AM NOT QUESTIONING YOUR AUTHORITY. WE WILL COMPLY WITH WHATEVER ORDER YOU CHOOSE TO GIVE.

...WE MOVE ON PRIMARY TARGET. REXALL. THEN A FINAL SWEEP OF THE AREA.

YES, SIR. WHATEVER YOU SAY.

LET'S *MOVE*!

YOU JUST HOLD ON. JUST HOLD ON. I'LL COME BACK FOR YOU.

SHOULDER'S NO GOOD. WON'T BE ABLE TO USE MY SLING.

NO. GUN'S NO GOOD.

HAVE TO USE THE *RAIN*.

IT'S SO LOUD IT'LL DROWN OUT ANYTHING QUIETER THAN A GUNSHOT.

THEY CALL IT THE *ROOF OF THE WORLD.*

THAT'S WHAT THE NATIVES CALL IT.

THEY THINK THE FOREST IS THE WHOLE WORLD AND FOR THEM IT IS.

FIVE LEFT.

AND MORETTI.

RAIN'S SO LOUD.

I HAVE A CHANCE.

BRAKK

BRAKABRAKABRA

MORETTI-- NO--I'VE GOT HER--

CHKCHAKK

KRAKKk

COLONEL MORETTI. YOU ARE UNDER ARREST.

DETAINED WITHOUT BAIL-- FACING CHARGES OF TREASON INCLUDING THE BRUTAL MURDER OF THE FIRST LADY--

--AND WITH THE ATTEMPTED ASSASSINATION OF PRESIDENT REXALL.

ON THE EVE OF A SPECIAL ELECTION, REXALL IS SHOWN LEADING IN EVERY POLL NATIONWIDE...

LIEUTENANT **WASHINGTON** TO SEE YOU, COLONEL.

LIEUTENANT. SHE MADE LIEUTENANT. I SHOULD'VE KNOWN. SEND HER ON IN. WHY THE HELL NOT.

YOU KNOW WHAT KIND OF PLACE I GREW UP IN, COLONEL. A LOT OF PEOPLE I KNEW ENDED UP IN PRISON, JUST LIKE YOU.

ONE REAL GOOD FRIEND I HAD WHEN I WAS A **KID**, HE GOT **FRAMED** FOR **MURDER**. ENDED UP FACING THE **DEATH PENALTY**.

THEY WERE GOING TO USE AN ANTIQUE **ELECTRIC CHAIR** ON HIM, NOT A **FIRING SQUAD** LIKE THE ONE YOU'RE FACING.

I VISITED HIM IN HIS CELL. HE ASKED ME FOR MY **BELT** AND I GAVE IT TO HIM.

LIKE I SAID, I WAS JUST A **KID**. I DIDN'T KNOW WHY HE WANTED IT UNTIL THE NEXT **MORNING**.

I GUESS THE WAITING WAS THE WORST OF IT FOR HIM.

DON'T GO. I DON'T WANT TO BE ALONE WHEN I DO IT.

YES, SIR.